WOMEN IN METAL FROM THE 1960S TO NOW

Wicked Woman
Women in Metal from the 1960s to Now

By
Addison Herron-Wheeler

This book is dedicated to my mom, Ann Dexter Androla.

Addison Herron-Wheeler is a music journalist, fiction writer, and editor who lives in Denver, Colorado. Contact wickedwoman@gmail.com to get in touch about this book, and check out the website at wickedwomanbook.com.

Hannah Swann is a graphic designer and illustrator who graduated from Virginia Commonwealth University in 2012. Art has always been part of her life, and now she aims to use her work to inspire and motivate social justice and the feminist movement. <u>HannahSwann.com</u>

Sarja Hasan is a graphic designer by profession and a photographer by hobby. She has been giving back to the underground punk and metal scenes by documenting band performances for the last decade. She is from Richmond, Virginia and now lives in Brooklyn, New York.

contact e-mail: sarja.hasan@gmail.com

Table of Contents

Author's Note

When I first had the idea for this book, I was taking a Women's Studies course called Women and Music. We were asked to choose a genre of music and talk about how women factored in: were they accepted, were they major players, did they meet with some sort of resistance over the years?

I chose to research women in metal, since I was already familiar with the genre. But when I started looking into the history of female participation in heavy metal, my mind was blown. The story was so compelling that I decided to write a book. I didn't want it to be like *Choosing Death* or any of the other books about metal out there. I don't mention every female musician or limit myself to an exclusively musical perspective. I wanted to tell the story of women in this particular musical genre throughout its relatively brief but colorful history. This narrative explores everything from the unacknowledged contributions of women in the early days of metal to the many roles women fill today, spotlighting along the way some famous, not-so-famous, and infamous participants in this scene.

And finally, I wanted to find connections between the experiences of modern women in an unorthodox genre to those of traditional female musicians in earlier times. Woven through this chronology are references to "the story of women in their relation to music," as Sophie Drinker subtitled her groundbreaking *Music and Women*, one of the books that inspired me to write my own.

Cast aside, at least for the time it takes to read this book, the multilayered divisions in the metal scene and the feminist community, and remember why you originally were drawn to women's issues, or how you felt when you heard heavy music for the first time. Then read on to discover the complex and fascinating relationship between women and heavy metal.

-Addison Herron-Wheeler

"Her incantations abound."

- Coven, "Wicked Woman" – *Witchcraft Destroys Minds and Reaps Souls*

Introduction

"It is in the presence of death that a woman's singing is called to its highest functioning. To the primitive mind, death is rebirth into another world... Women...are generally called upon to beat the drum of life, to act out the mimicry of birth, to pour the libation, to swing, to dance, to wave flowers and green branches, to tell the history of the departed, to wail, and especially to create and sing dirges."

-Sophie Drinker, *Music and Women*

The purpose of this book is to chart the history of female participation in the world of underground metal, from its inception in the 1970s to the present day. Over almost half a century, the genre has become a culture unto itself, with its own roster of gods and goddesses, as well as its own creation myths, and so I begin with the story of the heavy metal band Coven, fronted by a young woman named Jinx Dawson.

My inspiration to compare early civilizations to the culture of underground metal music, and to view the subject of women in metal from a feminist perspective, came from reading an extraordinary work of scholarship by an unlikely author. Sophie Drinker was a non-academic amateur musician who combined history, anthropology, and musicology to write *Music and Women*, a book that is still difficult to categorize, over sixty years after it first appeared. In a bold and sometimes defiant voice, she describes a time when women were leaders of religious ceremonies, creators of lyrics and melodies, and honored members of society. This way of life was wiped out by the rise of patriarchal civilizations, but traces of pagan goddess culture remained preserved in traditional song and dance. Drinker devoted decades of her life to finding and documenting these traces, and in the process developed her own feminist philosophy, one which remains relevant to the female experience in the 21st century.

In the pages that follow, Sophie Drinker's revolutionary ideas will be given new voice, and the history of women in extreme music will be retold, beginning with the saga of metal's original occult frontwoman, Jinx Dawson. In her time she stood alone, a witchy anomaly with a fierce and distinctly female sound among the men of proto-metal, but soon other women took up the cry and echoed it by making heavy music, through the decades and around the world. It was Jinx who first raised the sign of the horns, taking an ancient gesture associated with magic and making it her own before bestowing it upon an entire musical genre as an immediately recognizable symbol. Jinx not only performed a song entitled "Black Sabbath" while Ozzy and company were still calling themselves Earth, she and her band enacted the entire forbidden ritual onstage at their concerts, for Coven was an actual practicing coven, and the bond between their music and their beliefs was not a gimmick. But after the release of their first album, a twist of fate cost them their place in the musical vanguard. That void was quickly filled by Black Sabbath, and groups like Iron Maiden and Judas Priest, all purveyors of male-centered rock music, became the kings of heavy metal, eventually spawning multiple offspring, including death metal, black metal, and other genres more geared towards men than women.

But this is also the story of how women never left the metal scene, even though they had to endure being pushed aside and under-appreciated, and ultimately how they are reclaiming their place today by turning to the past. This is the story of how the cycle came about -- the story of women in heavy metal music.

Illustration of Jinx Dawson by Hannah Swann

Chapter One

Jinx Dawson and the Goddess Tradition:

The Rise of Heavy Metal

If witchcraft all the fools condemn,
It turns around and crushes them.
When good has been twisted,
When good has been killed,
Then love is resisted and blood will be spilled.

-Coven, "Black Sabbath" – *Witchcraft Destroys Minds and Reaps Souls*

Esther Jinx Dawson was born in Indianapolis in 1950. She survived a difficult delivery, but her twin was stillborn. Her mother chose her middle name in honor of the attending physician, a Dr. Jinks, and the alternate spelling in honor of 1940s supermodel Jinx Falkenburg. The name's supernatural connotations were no accident, because although the Dawson family was wealthy and well-respected, they were also "a lineage of Occult Adepts," as Jinx herself has called them, with many esoteric interests and memberships in secret societies, including the Ancient Order of Druids. Her nanny, a Creole woman with a background in hoodoo, introduced her to other hidden traditions and the sign of the horns, an ancient hand gesture associated with magic.

Trained in opera as well as the occult, Jinx considered herself a professional musician as well as a "ceremonial magician of the left-hand path" at an early age. While still in her teens, she decided to combine her love of music with her love of mysticism to start a rock band that would showcase her impressive voice and her occult beliefs.

"I came up with the name Coven because I had done extensive reading on the occult and loved classic horror films," she told Steve Hoffman of Steve Hoffman Music Forums. "I was very interested in the paranormal, secret societies, the black arts, and I knew the name Coven meant a band of thirteen witches. Remember, I was doing this at the tail end of the peace, love, hippie years, and the mood of the country at the time was getting darker and chaotic with so many assassinations, rioting against the Vietnam War and such, so I thought people would be interested in the ideas I was into. And [with] my opera background, I wanted to put these ideas into the music [to] do a kind of Gothic rock opera, theater, something no one had ever done before."

Jinx recruited bassist Oz Osbourne, guitarist Chris Neilson, Rick Durrett on keyboards, and drummer Steve Ross to form Coven in the late 1960s. The date of the band's formation is often given as 1969, but they were popular in their hometown and opening for groups like Vanilla Fudge, the Yardbirds, and Alice Cooper at least two years earlier; 1969 was actually the year they recorded their first album, *Witchcraft Destroys Minds and Reaps Souls*, for a big-name mainstream label, Mercury Records. They signed their contract with the company in their own blood.

The album was overtly Satanic, filled with songs about witches and devils, including "Wicked Woman," co-written by Jinx, "For Unlawful Carnal Knowledge," "Black Sabbath," "Dignitaries of Hell," and "Satanic Mass," a thirteen-minute-long recording of the entire ritual, which had become the signature first act of their concerts. Jinx presided in a long cloak, thrown off dramatically as she transformed from high priestess to rock singer. Her persona was part sorceress, part temptress, and her look was all contrast – black eye make-up on pale skin and long blonde hair on black velvet robes, a look that was both scary and sexy. However, the woman shown lying naked on the inside cover of *Witchcraft Destroys Minds and Reaps Souls* is not Jinx, as one of the myths about her would have it, but a look-alike blonde with arms spread and feet bound in a sacrificial pose, a chalice between her breasts and a human skull covering her crotch, surrounded by the members of the band in hooded robes, holding spooky-looking implements or giving the sign of the horns.

For a brief period after the album's release, Coven was gaining in sales, popularity and notoriety. When they performed, they drew not only avid fans, but protesters, hecklers, and usually a police presence. In Detroit, Jinx and the others were arrested. "They made us run through our whole stage show in the afternoon before the concert," she told Baron Saturday on his WNYU radio show, *Plastic Tales from the Marshmallow Dimension.* "They started pulling things off the stage, they took down the ritual table, and the candles, and finally, they said I couldn't speak any English to the audience." Later in the concert, things got worse. "We went into the fourth song, and I just said 'Happy All Hallows Eve, Detroit,' and we were pulled off the stage and detained at the Detroit police station."

Whether despite or because of their unconventional attitude and uncompromising Satanic leanings, Coven seemed headed for success, their potent mixture of devil worship and psychedelia designed to sell records in a market oversaturated with flower power. And if not for the murders committed by followers of Charles Manson in August of 1969, and the March 1970 issue of *Esquire* magazine, they might have had that success on their own terms.

The theme of the *Esquire* issue was "Evil Lurks in California." It contained one long article about the infamous Spahn Ranch, last home of the Manson family, along with other accounts and photographs of the questionable doings of Californians. In the middle of a minor story – not the Manson article – is a brief, anonymous man-in-the-street interview, three sentences in all, that changed the course of Coven's fortunes, and with it the path to stardom for women in metal.

"'Have you heard this new album?' says a Strip hippie. 'It's called *Witchcraft. Destroys Minds and Reaps Souls...* it says on the jacket...full of Black Mass stuff.'"

The rumors and misconceptions generated by that single reference are still circulating, most of them containing at least a component of truth. The one encountered most often on the internet has the *Esquire* article accompanied by a photo of Manson himself holding a copy of the album, and though apocryphal, it might as well have been factual, since Mercury Records, in anticipation of the anti-evil backlash, pulled the record from distribution entirely.

With nothing to promote and no new bookings coming in, Coven disbanded. Having relocated from Indianapolis to Los Angeles, its members managed to find work in various facets of the music industry, and during this time Jinx was asked to record the song "One Tin Soldier" for the soundtrack of the movie *Billy Jack*, another event that would prove to be a turning point in her career. The allegorical anti-war anthem, written by two male songwriters and originally recorded by a Canadian band, was a perfect vehicle for the imperious vibrato sound Jinx was capable of. She insisted that Coven, and not her own name, be listed in the credits of the film and the soundtrack recording, even though the other members were not involved. Her first version, done with studio musicians, made it to number 26 on the Billboard Top 100 in 1971, and a second version recorded by a reunited Coven charted twice in subsequent years.

The band went on to release two more albums, *Coven* for the MGM label in 1972 and *Blood on the Snow* for Buddah Records in 1974. They even made a music video for the title track of Blood on the Snow, years before MTV and the music video phenomenon, filled with archaic symbols and imagery that suggested their hearts still belonged to Satan, even if their earlier heavy sound veered toward the middle of the road as they struggled to find an alternative formula for success.

Meanwhile, another band interested in the occult started to take off, at first around their hometown of Birmingham, England, then in the U.S., and soon they were the worldwide phenomenon Coven could have been, with better luck and/or timing. This band, after a couple of false starts under other names, rechristened themselves Black Sabbath, a title shared by a track on *Witchcraft Destroys Minds and Reaps Souls*, Coven's debut album, which had been released several months prior to Earth's first appearance as Black Sabbath. Their first single was a cover called "Evil Woman," and they adopted a horror-inspired image to suit the new name.

There were more strange similarities between the two bands, and they didn't go unnoticed. The pioneering rock music critic Lester Bangs, in a disparaging *Rolling Stone* review of Black Sabbath's first album, referred to them as "something like England's answer to Coven." Jinx and her band even appeared on concert bills with their British rivals, and on at least one occasion manifested their irritation in a meaningful way. "A lot of bands at the time began to copy us," she told Baron Saturday in 2008. "I think the boys in Black Sabbath went a little too far. We were the ones that painted blood on their dressing room doors. It was at a show in Memphis, ironically, the birthplace of Elvis Presley."

Other semi-Satanic proto-metal bands were springing up, especially in the U.K., following the Sabbath model of all-male membership coupled with an image of over-the-top masculinity that had both sexual and sinister undertones, but no real connection to the occult. "I just don't think they wanted a girl in this position," Jinx said in the same 2008 interview. "I think they saw a man in this position. I think they couldn't picture a woman selling this black arts, heavy metal type of situation."

Starting in the 70s and for decades after Coven's downfall, heavy metal followed the all-male model almost exclusively. As metal grew into a force that couldn't be denied, the voices of women were almost drowned out by arena rock, power metal, supergroups, and flashy frontmen. For decades, it was a music scene unlike any other, where the overwhelming majority of the audience was male and everything, even hairstyles and fashion, was determined by men. There was no ongoing discussion of gender in those days, with the exception of the phrase often used to describe women in metal: "as good as a guy." Some chose to emulate the men, a viable approach as the 70s progressed and the trend toward androgyny prevailed. Regardless of how, female singers and musicians persevered and played on, refusing to concede the place won for them by Jinx Dawson, the original Wicked Woman.

Photo of Hysterics by Sarja Hasan

Chapter Two

Ram it Down:

In the Shadow of the Spandex Phallus

"You didn't like it
When I said no
You didn't want it
When I asked you to go

What could have led you
You to believe
Was it the skirt
Above my knees

Was it the way
I flicked my hair

Was it the way I said that
I did not care
You didn't mean that
That much to me
Now you'll be written out of my history"

- Girlschool, "Don't Mess Around" –
Legacy

Out of the simmering unrest in England in the early 1970s came a different scene, commonly known as the New Wave of British Heavy Metal (NWOBHM). This new type of metal grew more from the dissatisfaction of being born into a life of factory work and poverty than from any sense of unity with Satan and the occult. Instead of relying heavily on psychedelic tropes and bluesy roots, the bands in this movement took their influence from the fast-paced, harsh tones of punk rock, turning up the volume and distortion, and making for a much louder and more aggressive sound. Here is where heavy metal moves away from the rest of rock, firmly setting itself apart as a distinct genre.

The NWOBHM bands were mostly all-male, and they favored a decidedly hypermasculine attitude that had plenty of potential to alienate women. In his book *Running With the Devil: Power, Gender, and Madness in Heavy Metal Music*, Robert Walser discusses how this very male form of music provided a sense of bonding by promoting an intimate feeling of freedom and escape from society for men only, and an alternative way of validating masculinity. Metal lyrics were "fantasies of masculine virtuosity and control," about riding motorcycles, winning wars, pursuing conquests and exerting sexual prowess. As Walser describes it, "metal musicians typically appear[ed] as swaggering males, leaping and strutting about the stage, clad in spandex, scarves, leather, and other visually noisy clothing, punctuating their performances with phallic thrusts of guitars and microphone stands."

Ironically, some of these men performed their macho displays of virility wearing brightly colored leggings, flowing scarves, extreme hairstyles, and makeup. Partial explanations can be found in the fashions of the 70s and 80s, as well as a generally less-than-serious attitude that seemed to mock both genders. However, as Sophie Drinker points out, a similar phenomenon occurred in ancient Greece as goddess culture was being phased out: "Numbers of men performers had to dress as women, to cultivate women's voices and women's ways, and to sacrifice their own virile attributes to a silly feminization of their personalities."

But alongside all of this, there were multiple examples of women in the NWOBHM scene, as well as in the connected glam metal, power metal, and thrash scenes. Perhaps the most famous of these groups is Girlschool. Formed in 1975 as Painted Lady, they changed their name to Girlschool in 1978 and soon caught the attention of Lemmy Kilmister, who invited them to join Motörhead's tour the next year, leading to the release of their first album in 1980.

Guitarist and vocalist Kelly Johnson borrowed from her punk contemporaries to create a unique playing style which drew praise from heavy-hitting male guitarists and critics, and even won her an appearance on the cover of *Guitar Player* magazine in 1983, something few women had achieved. Girlschool never proclaimed themselves a feminist band, but their presence in the NWOBHM scene, not as a novelty but as an equal, was a message in itself. In their lyrics, they sometimes turned the tables of sexism, objectifying men and portraying themselves as hunters and stalkers, leading one reviewer to characterize their music as "stiletto in the groin."

Although they put out albums with Top 10 hits while working and touring just as hard as their male contemporaries, they never quite achieved the same level of popularity and financial success. Following Kelly Johnson's departure for a solo career, they bent to the pressure of selling out, attempting to appeal to a larger U.S. audience with a video for the song "Running Wild," featuring the band members wearing glam rock outfits that bore no resemblance to their former androgynous, punk-inspired look of leather jackets and jeans. The idea backfired with some fans who felt alienated by the sudden shift in image, but Girlschool stuck around, ultimately becoming the longest-running all-female group in rock history.

By the mid-70s, women in metal knew what they were up against, and Girlschool went into the industry knowing they would be lucky to gain recognition as musicians, and not just as girls who could actually play their instruments. They proved their musical prowess and earned respect with talent and ability, and also by trying to de-emphasize gender, an approach that would start a trend of women entering the arena swinging fiercely and insisting on equal footing with men, but rarely achieving it.

****

There were also American bands in the NWOBHM scene. One of the most familiar is Bitch, allegedly started in 1980 when Betsy Weiss, formerly the singer of a second-wave ska group called The Boxboys, answered an ad for a female vocalist placed by two male musicians who wanted to create a band called Bitch, with a heavy sound and a woman in front as the designated bitch. Betsy, who would eventually take the name Betsy Bitch, landed the job and got a crash course in current metal trends to supplement her knowledge of ska and punk. Bitch became the first female-fronted American metal band to sign a record contract, and one of the first bands on legendary label Metal Blade Records.

Bitch was known for their over-the-top live show and their use of bondage gear on stage. Like Girlschool, they inverted the paradigm of objectifying women. "We used to have all kinds of paraphernalia on stage, like a big tape board that had nails on it and I'd hang my whip and my riding crop and the handcuffs," Betsy said in an interview with *Metal Maidens*. "Then I'd do this thing where I'd bring this slave out on stage (he came out of a box, like a chest) and I would do an act with him on stage, sort of humiliate the hell out of him. It definitely gave the audience something to watch next to the music, that's for sure! But we had fun with that image and it definitely got people's attention. "Bitch recorded only three studio albums before breaking up in 1989, but because of their outrageous performances and Betsy's charisma, they have never faded into obscurity.

****

In the early 80s, there was a fine line between the New Wave of British Heavy Metal and what came to be known as glam metal, glitter metal, or hair metal. This genre took the look of the NWOBHM to extremes; bands in the scene wore heavy makeup, teased and dyed their hair, and sported tightly-fitting, flamboyant costumes. While the music itself was similar to the NWOBHM, with distorted guitars, screeching vocals, and heavy drumming, glam metal was catchier, more like pop music played using metal instruments, and aimed specifically at the MTV generation. Glam rockers, according to the *Feminist Legal Theory Blogspot*, "eschewed gender conventions and helped usher a new paradigm for the male rock star – the drug addled, sleazy, androgynous sex symbol." The blog goes on to say that the genre "helped legitimize androgynous imagery for subsequent rock sub-genres -- including goth and punk."

Warlock was a German glam metal band formed in 1982 with former members of the bands Snakebite and Beast. Doro Pesch had sung with various garage bands in Dusseldorf, and when she came on board as Warlock's frontwoman, she became the face of the band. Their look appealed to the hair metal world, but musically they were more on the heavy side, considered by some to be proto-thrash or speed metal. The band toured with metal icons like Judas Priest, Megadeth, and Dio, but never reached that level of acclaim. There were many lineup changes during their short time as a group, and Warlock broke up after recording three albums.

Another band that came out of the hair metal/glam metal scene was New York's Blacklace, formed in 1981 with Maryann Scandiffio on vocals. They toured with metal giants Manowar and famous cross-dressers Twisted Sister in Europe, and released two well-received studio albums. Indicative of what women had to endure in the 80s metal world is this review of Blacklace's 1984 album Unlaced, posted on *The Metal Observer* website by "Graham" in 2005, which takes the form of a reminiscence about Maryann's live performance. She is introduced as "a sexy figure," but Graham doesn't stop there. "Her trailer trash feathered bouffant, ready-as-hell lipstick smackers, heavy black eyeliner and spandex and chains have you lasciviously salivating and you know where your destination lies tonight, between the pumping thighs of this glorious Metal queen!" After listening to "March of the Black Witch" and several other diabolically-titled songs, the narrator starts to consider a young woman in the audience as his "next target," but with another song on the imaginary playlist, Maryann is "back on the dinner plate, but only for her ample breasts and pumping crotch."

****

Women aspiring to be metal musicians in the 1970s and 80s weren't given many choices. To make it in a man's world, they had to do exactly what the guys did, with the added expectation that they would run the gauntlet of sexism and misogyny without complaint. What is significant is that this also gave them the opportunity to own their musical and sexual powers with the same swaggering confidence as male performers. There is something uniquely sensual, and at the same time abrasive, in the way these women commanded attention, but it seemed their only option for survival and approval from a predominantly male audience.

Much of this era's onstage sexuality was inspired by the culture of bondage and the darker side of sex. This theater of exploration allowed Girlschool to write songs about hunting and controlling men, and created a space where Bitch could title their first album *Be My Slave*, and Betsy Bitch could simulate torture of male victims when the band performed. It was acceptable and all in good fun, but it was also sending out the message that women were not helpless victims, but strong and dominant, capable of wielding their female power and taking care of themselves.

The occult theme continued to appear lyrically, if not visually, during this period. Girlschool leaned toward more typical metal tropes as a rule, but also wrote songs like "Race with the

Devil" and "Hellrazor," and created a cover for their 1986 album *Nightmare at Maple Cross* that resembled a schlocky horror movie poster. Bitch took writing about bondage a step further with "Skullcrusher" on 1987's *The Bitch is Back*, and Warlock kept the cauldron flame alive, especially on their first two albums, *Burning the Witches* and *Hellbound*.

It was a confusing time for women in metal, as evidenced by masculinized, violent song titles, and by the adoption, at least for a while, of the androgynous or overtly masculine rock-star persona. But in the end, the era of the NWOBHM and glam metal proved to be a kind of trial by fire, and women emerged from it aware of their powers and in control of their legacy once again.

Photo of Scizophasia by Sarja Hasan

Chapter Three

Career of Evil:

Punk's Place in Metal and Feminism

"I plot your rubric scarab, I steal your satellite
I want your wife to be my baby tonight
I choose to steal what you chose to show
And you know I will not apologize
Your mine for the taking
I'm making a career of evil (repeat three times)

Pay me I'll be your surgeon, I'd like to pick your
brains
Capture you, Inject you, leave you kneeling in the
rain

I choose to steal what you chose to show
And you know I will not apologize
Your mine for the taking
I'm making a career of evil"
- Blue Öyster Cult, "Career of Evil" – *Secret Treaties* (lyrics written by Patti Smith)

"But whereas in primitive times women appear to have carried on their rites separately from men, as civilization developed, the tendency was for men and women to carry out their rites together. Many depictions of religious ceremonies represent a procession of men advancing from one side and of women from the opposite side, meeting before the altar in perfect equality."
- Sophie Drinker, *Music and Women*

In the 1970s, most noticeably in England and the U.S., a new counterculture was taking shape. Replacing peace and love with anarchy and anger, this scene turned away from the happy hippie aesthetic and embraced instead what was raw, brutal, and unadorned. The idea behind the punk scene was to get rid of the giant gap between those at the top, which meant rock musicians as well as political leaders, and the audience below. Rather than staging concerts in giant arenas and shielding themselves from the public, punk bands played in small clubs, hung out with the fans, and were in close contact with the independent zines springing up in this burgeoning do-it-yourself culture. In such an atmosphere, women were able to join and start bands, write music and write about music, and participate freely without gender factoring in as something to be overcome.

But in metal, also a newborn genre, walls were already going up that would keep women out. The two scenes stood in opposition to each other in those years, with the possibility of collaboration and crossover not yet explored, except in the tiny hotbed of creativity that was the downtown New York City art and music scene. Everybody knew everybody, free love was common, and so was collaboration; painting, photography, poetry, performance art, cabaret, and rock 'n' roll meshed in galleries, lofts, and clubs. And so it happened that punk's priestess, Patti Smith, and one of proto-metal's founding fathers, Allen Lanier, came together, with results that can be heard today on a list of legendary albums.

Patti is often referred to as a punk priestess, but the title is more than just an alliterative phrase to sum her up on the page. In ancient cultures, a priestess had ties to both royalty and commoners, but was set apart from the community, and served as a conduit to things secret and spiritual. Patti was definitely in the punk world, so much so that she will forever be identified with it, but she was not of it, having moved to New York to become not a rock star but an artist, then a poet. She took side trips into sculpture, photography, and performance art with her roommate Robert Mapplethorpe, acting and play writing with Sam Shepard, publishing, and even rock criticism, writing reviews for early magazines like *Creem*. It was with the idea of adding accompaniment to her first poetry reading at St. Mark's Church that she sought out guitarist Lenny Kaye, with whom she would later start the Patti Smith Group. Her brash attitude and androgynous look made her the embodiment of punk's egalitarian style, and her in-your-face act made her the subject of parody, but following the release of *Horses*, her influential debut album, she was suddenly taken seriously and admired far beyond Manhattan and the Bowery.

Wispy, wiry, and plain in person, graceful and ethereal in Mapplethorpe's photographs, onstage she was larger than life, a shamaness chanting the audience into a frenzy or a spitting, snarling demoness defying the gods. Her curiosity, intelligence, and talent attracted those with similar traits from the moment she arrived in the city in 1967; Janis Joplin and William Burroughs were among her famous friends, while Mapplethorpe, Shepard, Todd Rundgren, Tom Verlaine, and Allen Lanier were her on-and-off roommates, lovers, and collaborators in the late 60s and early 70s.

Allen was the co-founder, guitarist, and vocalist of the pioneering proto-metal group Blue Öyster Cult. They were the first band to use a symbol as a logo, theirs being the hook-and-cross sign associated with both mythology and alchemy, where it stands for lead – one of the heaviest metals. They were also the first to add an unnecessary umlaut to their name, two dots that have been widely copied, but they could have instituted a very different trend if they had made Patti Smith their frontwoman, a notion apparently considered in

1971, after her relationship with Allen Lanier began. Instead, several BÖC members shared singing duties, and Patti's contribution took the form of lyrics, some written exclusively for the band and some drawn from her own poetry. "Baby Ice Dog" appeared as a track on *Tyranny and Mutation* in 1973, "Career of Evil" on the next album, *Secret Treaties*, and 1976's *Agents of Fortune* contained "Debbie Denise" and "The Revenge of Vera Gemini," which lists Patti on vocals as well. Words for songs and poems came to her from the raunchiness of porn and rock 'n' roll, but just as often from sources that were esoteric, religious, or supernatural; her cryptic writing style and surreal subject matter were a good fit for a group that deliberately kept an air of mystery about them.

At the same time, Allen assisted Patti with her increasingly popular poetry gigs and with the writing and recording of her landmark album *Horses*, and the two records that followed. According to *Rolling Stone*, "Lanier co-wrote and played guitar on Smith's 'Elegie,' from *Horses*, and also contributed material and keyboard parts to *Radio Ethiopia* and *Easter*. The horse pin seen on Smith's jacket on the cover of *Horses* was a gift from Lanier." The strain of constant touring ended their romance in the late '70s, but not their musical exchange. BÖC had hits with two more songs penned by Patti, "Fire of Unknown Origin," and "Shooting Shark" in the early 80s.

Addressing a question concerning gender in a 1977 interview for *Acid Rock* magazine, she said this: "I don't think it's that guys are actually emotionally stronger, it's just that they usually have a stronger shield. You see, there has to be a better exchange from both sides. Guys have to learn to be a little more sensitive, to open themselves up a little more. And chicks have to sort of borrow some of that 'Kryptonite' guard that guys sometimes seem to have a monopoly on. Men and women could learn so much from each other if they'd only open their eyes."

****

Like Patti Smith, Wendy O. Williams arrived in New York City with no aspirations of rock stardom, but simply in need of a job. After dropping out of high school at sixteen and traveling for over a decade in America and Europe, in 1976 she auditioned for a radical art project/live sex show called Captain Kink's Theatre, and was hired by Rod Swenson, the man behind the idea, to perform as a dominatrix on stage. This marked the beginning of a partnership, both personal and professional, that would last for over twenty years.

Rod Swenson was a conceptual artist with an MFA from Yale, and Captain Kink's was a repertory company that put on a new live show every week in an old burlesque theater on Times Square, sort of a subversive *Saturday Night Live* for the downtown punk crowd. He also managed and shot videos for some of the new bands creating the scene at CBGB's, and soon he and Wendy decided to form their own group. In 1978 The Plasmatics their debut.

Their act was an assault, an over-the-top
,on of metal, punk, noise, chaos, nudity, and
violence, and it was a hit, soon outgrowing the
small New York clubs and playing to huge
audiences in large stadiums and arenas. Provocative
and profane, Wendy roared in a raspy voice, bared
her breasts (sometimes covering each nipple with an
X of electrical tape), simulated sex and
masturbation, and shot objects out of her vagina.
She accompanied herself on the chainsaw, ripping
through guitars, amplifiers, TVs, and cars, and
punctuated her songs with explosions, blowing up
anything in her path. Each performance was more
outrageous than the last, and Wendy O. Williams
became a sensation.

Rod Swenson granted a rare interview to
Vice magazine in 2012, in which he spoke about
Wendy publicly for the first time in the two decades
since her suicide: "Wendy, during the first several
years of her career was called 'the Queen of Punk
Rock.' Later, as we mixed (to the horror of some
our early fans) punk and metal, various magazines
started calling her the 'High Priestess of Metal,' but
she was also called the 'Queen of Shock Rock.' Part
of the assault on conformity and what we saw as
blind worshiping of consumerism was shocking to
people indoctrinated into it."

Transcending genres again, Wendy recorded
a cover of the country song "Stand by Your Man"
with Lemmy Kilmister of Motörhead in 1982. It
was released as one side of an EP, leading one
reviewer to characterize the duet as "one of hard

rock's greatest-ever middle fingers to the mainstream." On the B side, they swapped songs, with Lemmy singing the Plasmatics' "Masterplan," and Wendy belting out Motörhead's "No Class."

The Plasmatics went on to release seven albums, one of them entitled *Heavy Metal Priestess*, before breaking up in 1983. In January of that year, Wendy appeared on the alternative TV variety show *Night Flight*, weighing in on the subject of the female presence in the metal world. "Heavy metal has always been predominantly dominated by men," she said. "There are a lot of women out there with great heavy metal bands, but they persist to sing like pop singers, because that's what the industry encourages them to do. And I just want to be known as the heaviest woman in heavy metal. I'm singin' it out, just singin' it, and just spilling my guts every time I go on stage, every time I do an album. This is the only thing I know how to do, I'm true to myself, and I just give it everything I've got. I like heavy metal because it gives me the room to put all of my emotions into what I'm doing."

****

In the 1970s and 80s, when metal and punk were both young and raw, they tended to diverge rather than merge, with genre-crossing chapters in the careers of Patti Smith and Wendy O. Williams the notable exceptions. In addition to divisions between these categories of music, it is important to point out that divisions and distinctions between women and men were just beginning to erode at that time, with the advent of second-wave feminism and its establishment as a cultural force. In the culture at large, as well as the world of rock music, it was unusual for the sexes to achieve the high levels of collaborative equality reached by Patti Smith with Allen Lanier and Blue Öyster Cult, and Wendy O. Williams with Rod Swenson and The Plasmatics.

But in the lively punk universe, examples of such creative teamwork were not hard to find. The New York psychobilly punk group The Cramps, formed in 1976, was the brainchild of husband and wife Lux Interior and Poison Ivy. On the West Coast, John Doe taught his girlfriend Exene Cervenka to harmonize with his vocals and put her in front of X, the influential band he and Billy Zoom formed in 1977. Meanwhile, in London, entrepreneurial duo Vivienne Westwood and Malcolm McClaren molded four young customers of their shop into the Sex Pistols. Later, when two Pistols fans, Siouxsie Sioux and Steve Severin, took the stage in an impromptu performance, Siouxsie and the Banshees were born.

The critical and commercial success of these and other bands helped bring down the heavy metal walls for female musicians in the years to come. Female unity was also a contributing factor; however, these women were not motivated by feminism alone, but also by the strong bond they shared with their supportive male counterparts, and their powerful alliances left a mark on punk, metal, and gender stereotypes outside the world of underground music.

Photo of Bastard Deceiver by Sarja Hasan

Chapter Four

Princesses of Hell:

Women in Glam, Speed

and Thrash

I was the first - I am not the last
So face the dead - let's start it fast
Survive the mighty flash of thrash

Amps are roaring - power chords clash
Our razor blade edge - hammer the wizard
Double-bass pounds - for the metal blizzard
Wring your axe - to bomb the hall

Blood on my strings - until I fall

Princess of hell - Give it to me
Princess of hell - It's my decay
Princess of hell - For your body to smell

Holy Moses, "Princess of Hell" – *Disorder of the Order*

"When men took over the whole basic material of women's festivals, they made some remarkable changes. In the first place, they transformed them from religious rituals into great, popular shows, performed not in the sacred place but on a large stadium. In the second place, they took them entirely out of women's hands; numbers of men performers had to dress as women..."
- Sophie Drinker, *Music and Women*

As the era of the New Wave of British Heavy Metal reached its peak in the 1980s, the over-the-top theatrics of many bands were at an all-time high. Attending a Judas Priest show late in the decade, audiences expected to see singer Rob Halford ride onto a gigantic arena stage on a motorcycle, clad in custom-made black leather and surrounded by the glimmer of expensive pyrotechnics. Newly-formed bands who chose this extreme approach to showmanship created a genre that became known as hair metal, sometimes called glam metal or pop metal. Glam rock, similar in style but less heavy, put the emphasis on fashion, mixing spandex and leather with the cross-dressing aesthetic of trend-setting glam pioneer David Bowie.

Glam metal combined the two styles, and earned its alternate name, hair metal, from the dramatically teased and dyed hairstyles favored by male singers and musicians. This genre borrowed from glam rock musically as well, incorporating catchy hooks and other pop elements into the more aggressive sound of the NWOBHM. As visual fixtures, women were made somewhat redundant, yet there were some who made themselves part of the scene.

Perhaps the most famous example is Lita Ford, lead guitarist of The Runaways, the all-female group co-founded by Joan Jett in 1975. When The Runaways' rock sound started heading in a punk direction, Lita decided to pursue a solo career. Her long blond hair and tough-but-relatable charisma were perfect for attracting the hair metal crowd, but her main focus was her guitar playing. "I would go to shows like Johnny Winter and watch artists who played guitar and sang, like Jimi Hendrix," Lita told *The Examiner* in a 2013 interview. "That's who I was into, and I really wanted to establish myself as a female guitarist, and the only way to do it was like when I put out *Out For Blood*, which was my first solo album, it was a three-piece band like Jimi Hendrix, just bass, drums and guitar. So therefore there was nobody else to look at on the stage, so nobody could say …he's doing all the guitar playing."

Despite her instrumental skill, Lita felt she

was being forced into the role of sexy female rock star rather than being taken seriously as a songwriter and guitarist. After her first three solo albums failed to sell, she hired Sharon Osbourne's company to represent her. Ironically, considering that Sharon's husband is Ozzy Osboure who started Black Sabbath, Lita was advised to tone down the darker and more technical aspects of her image and sound. Her next album, *Lita*, did receive more acclaim, and contained a duet with Ozzy himself on "Close My Eyes Forever," which reached a stratospheric 8th position in the Billboard Top 100 songs.

As the popularity of hair metal music grew, the levels of innovation and talent seemed to diminish. Diehard metal fans, increasingly dissatisfied with the bloated mainstream metal industry, now discovered the band that had been there all along – the forefathers of speed metal, Motörhead. Already popular in the underground scene, and infamous for the sideburns and antics of their swaggering frontman, Lemmy Kilmister, Motörhead were admired for their straightforward, punk-influenced rock 'n' roll sound, as well as the speed and intensity of their riffs. As metalheads took a cue from their punk cousins – the experts on overthrowing an engorged rock empire – speed metal, which had been around in some form for several years, began to take off. Bands such as Anvil, Venom, and early Metallica embraced the concept by playing faster than any metal bands had dared in the past. They generated excitement by interacting with the audience, turning the arena-rock model upside down by encouraging mosh pits and stage diving.

This newfound scene quickly evolved into thrash metal, a style similar to speed metal but more refined, with added attention to musical technique. Metallica, Anthrax, Slayer, and Megadeth, also known as "The Big Four," founded it and gave it character with their punk-influenced riffs and brutally fast guitars. This is also the genre that introduced double-bass pedal drumming to metal, a trope that would go on to characterize death metal and other extreme forms. Thrash also reintroduced the guitar solo and other technical elements from the NWOBHM era, injecting them into the small-club atmosphere and giving them new life. Metal bands and fans began to embrace the do-it-yourself ethos of punk, spreading the word about shows via hand-drawn fliers and word of mouth and trading cassette tapes to hear new music rather than relying on the radio.

Although thrash did not have the same amount of female participation as the early punk scene, there were definitely more women in the audiences of thrash shows, and more than just a few of the musicians they came out to support were female. A premier representative was Ann Boleyn, outspoken frontwoman of Hellion, a Los Angeles thrash band. She did a short stint with The Runaways, as well as a few other less successful girl groups in the late 70s, and also landed a gig with KROQ-FM radio station in Los Angeles, hosting a show that featured metal and punk bands. As the playlist began to focus more and more on new metal music, it was christened "Speed Metal Hell," after a term that Boleyn herself came up with to describe the faster, more aggressive brand of metal.

Ann joined Hellion in 1982 as a keyboardist, but when a suitable lead singer for the band failed to materialize, she and guitarist Ray Schenck shared vocals. She made no secret of her interest in witchcraft and the occult, supposedly leading to the abrupt departure of original bassist Peyton Tuthill that same year. Like Jinx Dawson of Coven, Ann claims a family connection to the dark side; in a 2002 interview, she said that her grandfather, a doctor, was a friend of Aleister Crowley, and that her other grandfather taught her to use a divining rod when she was a child. "When I was eighteen I worked with Dr. John Brooker, who was doing government-sponsored experiments in out-of-body travel," she told *Ballbuster Hard Music*. "In the Hellion song 'Break the Spell' I sing 'Magic is the power of the science of the mind'... Have I practiced magic? Absolutely! It is my religion."

The first incarnation of Hellion released a few albums on the Mystic Records label. Then, with the support of metal contemporary Ronnie James Dio, they left Mystic to sign with Roadrunner Records, which released a Dio-produced Hellion single, "Run for Your Life," on a compilation album. The song had some radio play in the U.S. and abroad, but no record deal followed, and in 1985, the male members of Hellion split with Ann and hired a male vocalist. She retained custody of the band name, however, and continued to perform with an all-new lineup.

Ann pulls no punches when asked about her early days in the music business. "People have no clue what it was like to be a female in a band in the 1970s or 1980s," she said in an interview with *Steel and Fire*. "In the 1970s, everybody viewed the female rockers as virtual prostitutes. If there were any laws to protect female performers from sexual harassment, they were not enforced. I remember hearing the manager of The Runaways brag about how two members of the band had been auctioned off at a holiday party for Mercury Records. This was 'normal' back then. Nobody batted an eye. It was 'no big deal.' People forget that the girls in The Runaways were underage. Joan Jett and Sandy West were fourteen or fifteen. Lita and I were a couple of years older, but we were still under eighteen. We were all basically and legally 'children.' If those things happened today, there would be huge lawsuits."

In the same interview, she addressed the issue of gender in Hellion's breakup. "Most guys had problems with the idea [of] having a girl in their band. Today it is considered 'cool,' but back then it was a totally different story. No matter how good I was, 'the guys' were always trying to find a 'guy' to replace me. They just thought that people wouldn't accept them as a 'real band.' ...There was a real stigma to having a girl singer, and it was not good. In LA during the 1980s, the only bands who were really successful and who had a girl singer played hard rock or pop music. Most all of the bands who were signed in LA during the 1980s had a simple formula; they were mostly all white guys with big hair."

****

An interesting figure who entered the scene at this time was The Great Kat, aka Katherine Thomas. Kat attended Juilliard for classical music with an emphasis on strings, and graduated to begin touring and performing classical pieces. Soon, she got bitten by the metal bug and began to perform thrash and speed metal covers of classical songs, usually on electric guitar, but occasionally playing the violin. In 1987, her first album, *Worship Me or Die*, appeared, followed by *Beethoven on Speed* in 1990. She started billing herself as "The High Priestess of Shred Guitar," and critics agreed, among them *Guitar One* magazine, who listed her as one of the "Fastest Shredders of All Time."

Despite her overwhelming musical talent, she also relied heavily on sex appeal to sell her image, appearing on stage in outrageous outfits and dominatrix gear. "I'll explain to you the exact theory behind The Great Kat's 'provocative' image," she said, speaking about herself (as always) in the third person in an interview with *Rock Eyez*. "The Great Kat is taking [the] highly complex classical masterpieces of Beethoven, Bach, Paganini, Mozart, Vivaldi (music that is out of the intellectual reach of the average idiot) and bringing these masterpieces to them, by wearing provocative clothes, leather, vinyl, whips and chains, so as to distract the morons from the musical complexities of the genius composers, by targeting directly to their penises – which is where their brains are located!" Proving that she is more than just a novelty, The Great Kat began her act in 1986 and is still performing and recording wickedly fast covers of classics today.

Another force to be reckoned with in this scene was Leather Leone, of Rude Girl and Chastain. Leather took to the stage in the early 80s as a vocalist, along with her friend Sandy Sledge on drums, to start an all-female metal band called Rude Girl in the San Francisco area. They were well-received and played alongside such well-known Bay Area thrash bands as Megadeth and Suicidal Tendencies. Although they got plenty of gigs and almost landed a record deal, Rude Girl broke up before they could officially release an album.

Then, in 1994, Leather was recruited for Chastain, the group put together by Shrapnel Records to showcase the talents of David T. Chastain, guitarist of a little-known Cincinnati band, CJSS. The label recognized major talent in David, and decided to pair him with other formidable musicians to form a supergroup. These included guitarist Pat O'Brian, who would later go on to be in Cannibal Corpse, future members of the Alice Cooper and King Diamond bands, and Leather Leone on vocals. "Those were harsh days for female performers," she recalled in an interview with unratedmagazine.com, "...[but] in all honesty...I don't remember that it was harsher on me than any guy who was starting out. Sledge and Chastain have different views on that. For me, I have just always tried to express my inner being through my voice. I wasn't trying to become anything [other] than the best I could be! As far as the women in metal today: I am so fucking proud of them! They have all stepped up!!!"

Sabina Classen, another formidable female from this era, was a member of the German thrash metal band Holy Moses. The group formed in 1981, featuring Sabina on vocals, and her husband at the time, Andy Classen, on guitar. Although the group never reached the status of their American contemporaries, they successfully released several albums, went on tour, and even hosted a television program called *Mosh*, a German version of the American show *Headbangers Ball*. When the band broke up in 1994, Classen went on to start another band, Temple of the Absurd. After a short stint with them, she reformed a new version of Holy Moses, who are still touring and playing shows today.

Holy Moses have been touted as a band well ahead of their time; their sound was extreme for the 80s, foreshadowing death and black metal. "Yes, I really know now, that I was the very first growling and extreme music woman in metal," said Sabina in an interview with *Femme Metal Webzine*. "I think this is also a milestone and something really special. I feel great with it, if anybody – male or female – got from my music and my strength, [the] power and energy …to be happy."

The 1980s and early 90s were an exciting time for metal music in general, as well as for female participation. The emergence of both a strong underground scene and a media-driven mainstream metal scene brought increased attention and helped women establish their right to sing, scream, and shred with the men. Soon they would go on to reclaim their place as mistresses of dark music and become major players in the world of heavy metal.

Photo of Occultist by Sarja Hasan

Chapter Five

She was Asking for It:

Women in Death Metal

I wrapped my hands around her neck
Squeezing out her breath
Eyes rolled back in her head
Clawing at my skin
I know now it's not my fault
She was asking for it

   - Cannibal Corpse, "She Was Asking for It"
– The Bleeding

"As an art form, [women's dirges] evolved from the cry of childbirth, and for musical existence, depend upon a sound natural only to women. Dirges and laments are noticeably absent from the repertoire of primitive men. It is the mother's business to bring life, even in death."
- Sophie Drinker, *Music and Women*

Perhaps the most compelling and contradictory chapter in the female history of heavy metal is the story of death metal. For the most part, this has been a genre made by men and for men, relying on extreme aggression, violence, and brutality not only as a musical style, but also as a source of lyrical material, with songs in which women are victims of horrific, graphic crimes not uncommon. However, both historically and currently, there are many noteworthy female contributors to the death metal scene, and while they do meet with some resistance, there is still much support from many of their male peers.

****

Death metal started as a natural progression of the heavy tendencies of thrash and speed metal. Faster playing and more extreme vocals were part of it, but Possessed and Death, two U.S. bands that formed in the early 1980s, were also inspired by the morbid themes and Satanic imagery of thrash greats Slayer and Venom. These bands took thrash to the next level, incorporating guttural vocals more akin to growls and screams than actual singing, plenty of tremolo picking, i.e. very fast guitar and bass, and maximum amounts of double-bass drumming, which eventually evolved into the drum technique known today as blast beats. From these beginnings, death metal spread around the world, detonating an underground explosion that would reverberate for decades to come.

By the early 90s, Cannibal Corpse, Deicide, and Morbid Angel were some of the biggest names in American death metal. Both Deicide and Morbid Angel were famous for occult and anti-Christian lyrics, themes already familiar in the metal world. In fact, aside from an increased fascination with death and the body, most early death metal bands' lyrics revolved around familiar subjects, with the exception of Cannibal Corpse.

This band from Buffalo caused a sensation outside the boundaries of metal due to the extremely graphic nature of their material; almost every song is about someone being brutally murdered, and usually, the victim is female. When Edgar Allan Poe wrote that "the death of a beautiful woman is, unquestionably, the most poetical topic in the world," he was paving the way for the extreme lengths to which Cannibal Corpse went with this topic. Their catalog, which includes such inflammatory titles as "She Was Asking for It," "Entrails Ripped From a Virgin's Cunt," and "Fucked With a Knife," gained them so much negative attention that the U.S. Senate, along with Germany, Australia, and various cities worldwide, attempted to ban them from playing. With titles like these, Cannibal Corpse brought the underlying misogyny of the metal world to the forefront, giving other bands permission to emulate them, and thus creating what would seem to be the perfect setup for a movement devoid of women altogether. For a variety of reasons, though, this turned out not to be the case.

****

In an interview for Albert Mudrain's *Choosing Death*, Jo Bench, bassist of the death metal band Bolt Thrower, stated, "I think there are more women in the scene now than when I started in 87, but I never thought 'Oh, no, I'm the only girl.' If I did, I don't think it lasted five minutes. I found it easier just to get on with it and let the music do the talking." Bolt Thrower, formed in 1986, were one of the first British death metal bands to gain international fame, and are known for their fantasy-inspired lyrics, with an emphasis on warfare and weaponry. Jo came on board in 1987, and quickly proved that she could hold her own in such a masculinized setting. According to *Loudwire*, Bolt Thrower's intense sound "could never be the same without Jo's pummeling bass tone and ...playing style." While she acknowledges that there were hardly any women in the scene when she got involved, she doesn't attempt to trade on being one of the first women in death metal, preferring acceptance on equal terms to a high feminist profile.

There are many female death metal singers who also try to keep the focus on the music and avoid gender distinctions. Angela Gossow, singer of the Swedish band Arch Enemy, was quoted in *Choosing Death* as saying "Adding the clean female voice in Arch Enemy's sound would make it totally cheesy. I shouldn't have to do that just because of my gender." Angela joined the band as a replacement for original vocalist Johan Liiva, an established male singer who had staked a claim in German death metal, and from the start it was clear that she was up to the job. In a 2009 interview with *Enslain* magazine, she revealed the secret of her throaty growl. "I'm a mezzo-soprano, I'm not even an alto, or contra-alto, which is a really deep female voice. But somehow the way my muscles work, because the growling is not really vocal chords, it's the false chords next to them, they do what I want them to do, and they produce that sound. A lot of people don't know how to use their false chords."

Another European group, the Spanish death metal band Haemorrhage, started in 1990 as a three-piece, and subsequently went through several lineup changes and recorded several demos. Their big break came in 1994, when they finally settled on a solid lineup, which included founding guitarist and vocalist Luisma's girlfriend Ana on guitar, and their promo tape landed them a deal with Morbid Records. In the years that followed, Haemorrhage rose in popularity, with several albums and multiple world tours to their credit.

Ana and Luisma's relationship and subsequent marriage have led to the inevitable questions about her inclusion in the band. During an interview with the blog *Infernal Dominion*, Luisma gave this answer: "Including Ana in the band was something 'accidental' ...we had no bass player. Ana was my girlfriend (and now my wife) and sometimes she came to see our rehearsals and then we jammed together, so I knew she was an amazing guitar player. So I just asked her if she was also interested in playing bass on a couple of shows. After those shows there were others who wanted her in their bands, but our bassist, Ramon left his job and returned to our town so Ana stayed in the band as guitarist and Ramon took on bass. I think Ana has proved she's not only an exotic female element in the band. She's a talented guitar player, and she's underrated because in this style she can't show all that she can do." From this and other interviews, it is clear that the other members of Haemorrhage value Ana's contributions as a strong female musician as highly as Luisma does, and the band's long-lived success is proof that their fans agree.

Unfortunately, not all women in death metal have had positive experiences as part of a male-dominated band. In 2010, the Glasgow-based band Cerebral Bore replaced a male singer with a woman, Simone "Som" Pluijmers, a native of the Netherlands. Almost immediately, fan and label response to their music went from enthusiastic to positively exuberant. Simone's stage presence was terrific, and she had a death growl that could shatter concrete. In fact, her voice was so good that Cerebral Bore were suspected of layering their vocals or using some other studio tricks, not because their singer was a woman, but because it simply seemed impossible for any human voice to do what hers was doing on its own.

The band recorded a full-length album with Simone, immediately picked up in 2011 by metal label Earache Records. They toured extensively, even released a few music videos, and seemed poised to attain high status in the death metal universe. Then, in November 2012, just 24 hours before the start of a U.S. tour with three big-name death metal bands, Simone unexpectedly quit. Cerebral Bore's guitarist, Paul McGuire, released an official statement on Facebook announcing that she had "walked out," implying that she was unstable and had left because she couldn't handle the pressure. He elaborated in an interview with *Blistering* when asked if the band anticipated this turn of events, saying, "Pretty much, yeah. We could tell because she was acting weird, then she disappeared. At the end of the day, we need to keep pushing forward. We've been a band a lot longer before we gave Som the opportunity that we gave her."

But Simone tells a different story. Her online response to Paul's account of her departure read, "I'm sorry but I was too unhappy with him and had to leave. There was more going on than this, but if he's gonna start bullshit then I'm more than happy to tell you guys the truth. I had to do this for me and thought about fans, etc. It was a difficult decision …But for the best …Living with someone you're scared of is not good, guys, I hope you understand. Please take care."

Internet message boards, which earlier had run rampant with comments about her lack of femininity – wondering, for example, why she "was trying to dress like a teenage boy," and exhorting her to "make herself more sexy" – were on fire with speculation about what really happened, who was to blame, and what effect it would have on the band's future. "It was after she joined that the band's popularity skyrocketed," was the opinion of *No Clean Singing*; however, Simone's vocal prowess was not cited as the reason: "And those things didn't happen because the band's music suddenly became better …She and her now-former bandmates elevated their profile dramatically because of her gender." The article goes on to repost an anonymous Facebook comment: "'And there goes 85% of Cerebral Bore's fanbase. Better hurry up and sew a vagina onto one of the remaining members.'"

The more things change, the more they stay the same; women in metal still face such sexist attitudes, and probably will in the years to come. Ms. Anthropia of the *Feminist Headbanger Blog* remains optimistic, though, and hopes that the raw energy contained in the genre itself might be a catalyst for improvement. "Metal provides a much needed release for some fans, validation for others, whose voices may not be heard or valued. Metal has enormous potential to be transformative for that reason – to change the conversation. There is TONS of feminist potential there."

****

The urge to contemplate and even glorify death is an ancient one. Many traditional religious practices recognize and incorporate this human need in ritual, art, and song. In such a way, it is believed possible to gain a deeper understanding of what it means to live, as well as to die, and perhaps, as some cultures hold, to transcend or reach enlightenment. There was a time when women wrote and conducted the rites of death, often excluding men altogether or allowing them to participate only under certain conditions. Even after the demise of the goddess culture, women were understood to have closer spiritual ties to death because of the physical experience of birth; the reasoning was that those who brought life from the spirit world into the realm of flesh and blood were naturally intended to be the ones to preside over the journey back. Sophie Drinker recognized and reaffirmed these ideas when she wrote, "To the primitive mind, death is rebirth into another world. Because women bring life, they are needed to assist the spirit along its destined path."

It is ironic that death metal and black metal, two closely related genres with histories of being unfriendly to women, also profess an idealized admiration of ancient pagan cultures. Male musicians, searching for alternatives to a world they despised and nostalgic for a past reminiscent of the pagan way, still often chose to ignore the existence of the goddess tradition.

Photo of Arctic Flowers by Sarja Hasan

Chapter Six

Freezing Moon:

Women in Black Metal

come to me, i live for thee
come to me, i live for thee Satan
my sacrificions are for you
take me, take me Satan

on the edge of my life, i'm looking down
but i don't wanna fall down without meaning
so i take you, take you with me
i'm always in this empty room, but never alone
i'm always in this empty room, but never alone

i'm always in this hollow body, captured,
but never weak

you gave me this strength, power,
supernatural ability
to destroy everything on my way

come to me, i live for thee
come to me, i live for thee Satan
take me, take me Satan
        - Anguished, "Come to Me Satan" – *Cold*

     "I have the magical treasure
     I have supernatural power
     I can return to life."
     -Kwakuitl song, as qtd. In *Music and Women*

       Running parallel to the death metal scene is the black metal scene, which started in Norway in the early 1990s. Black metal was inspired by the rise of death metal, and is in fact very similar in style, although more heavily influenced by the demonic growls of the late thrash band Venom, who have been credited with creating the genre. Stylistically, black metal is more chaotic and less formulaic than death metal, and often features high-pitched, screechy vocals instead of low growls, extremely blasting drums, and harsh distortion on guitar. The genre is also known for conveying a corpse-like and sometimes demonic image, relying on black-and-white face paint, extreme outfits, and outrageous behavior – both on and off the stage – to provide the scene with a sense of otherness and infamy.

Among the pioneering bands of this genre in Norway, there was a strong sentiment that Christianity was an evil and destructive force which had erased their country's pagan heritage. As a result, a small group of black metal followers chose to burn down ancient churches built by early Christian missionaries, forever marring irreplaceable historical landmarks and giving black metal a very bad name. Some of the early groups associated with these church burnings, such as Mayhem, Burzum, and Bathory, were characterized by a pro-National Socialist stance and a hatred of society as a whole.

During this chapter in black metal's history, women had little or no place in the scene except as fans, but as the genre later distanced itself from its tainted roots, its bleak imagery began to appeal more to women as well as men. While black metal shares the raw power and aggression of death metal, it is more mystically pagan than overtly masculine, perhaps because it was originally intended to inspire Norwegian metalheads to remember their ancestral roots, and thus a space was made in an unlikely metal genre for witchlike imagery and dark, goddess-inspired feminism, where women could be as brutal and merciless as men, but also embrace their feminine attributes.

****

Given the elitist attitude prevalent in the early years of black metal, it is no surprise to find few female names associated with it; essentially, if you were not a man of Scandinavian ancestry, there was no need to apply. It took a trailblazing young Korean-American woman to make headway on that almost impenetrable front. From there, Kimberly Goss went on to influence a number of genres and inspire other women to break into a predominantly male world.

At a young age, Kimberly was already listening to heavy metal, raised by her mother on the likes of Alice Cooper, Slayer, and Whitesnake. She was just fifteen when she joined the Chicago metal act Avernus as their singer, and soon she began playing keyboards as well. "With Avernus, I was already the only female member and it just felt natural," she told *Metal Maidens*. "Ever since I was younger, I really only hung out with boys. I did …boy things, like play baseball. I didn't really like to wear dresses or anything like this. I was pretty much into sports, when I was a young girl. Also, this music scene is very male dominated, so I just assumed there's not that many women listening or involved in this scene anyway – at least that's what I thought at the time – so it really [was] natural and didn't feel weird at all."

In 1996, Kimberly relocated to Norway at the invitation of the members of Ancient, one of the original Norwegian black metal bands, although not one involved in the church burnings. During her brief stint with them, Ancient gained recognition as one of the first bands to incorporate haunting female vocals and background keyboards into their sound. After recording one album, she left Ancient to join Therion, a Swedish group with a more experimental musical attitude and some commercial success. Continuing her nomadic career, she went on tour with Dimmu Borgir as a keyboardist, during which time she conceived the idea for another band, created in 1999 with In Flames guitarist Jesper Stromblad and called Sinergy.

The two recruited other musicians for Sinergy, including Alexi Laiho of the Finnish band Children of Bodom, with whom Kimberly moved once again, this time to Finland, where a second version of Sinergy was formed. Together for several years, Kimberly and Alexi were married in 2002 and separated in 2004, although they remained close and continued working together.

Recently, Kimberly has ventured into the mainstream with various projects. In 2011, one of her songs was featured on an ABC Family network television show, and since then she has scored background music for several other shows. After the birth of her daughter, she returned to the Chicago area, where she is currently an instructor in the "Little Wing" program for young children at the School of Rock in Plainfield, Illinois.

****

The story of Onielar, a contemporary of Kimberly Goss, is a different one, and perhaps more representative of traditional black metal. Onielar has been the frontwoman of one band, Darkened Nocturn Slaughtercult, since their inception in 1997. Still active after twenty years, they are one of the only true black metal bands to hail from Germany, although Onielar herself is of Polish descent. *Loudwire* calls her "one of the most overlooked women in all of heavy metal" and "the most terrifying female frontwoman on the planet."

Onielar performs in full corpse paint, complete with chalk-white face, cadaver-like black eye makeup, and a signature blood-red chin. With blond hair falling past her waist and elbow-length spiked cuffs on her muscular arms, she resembles a ghoulish Viking queen as she commands the stage in an intense show, complete with blood and giant inverted crosses. Her piercing, aggressive vocals stand out against the background of the band's chaotic music, which she described as "a real, honest product of true thoughts," in an interview with *Lords of Metal* ezine. "The corpse paint is also used with utmost conviction. Even the blood is real, as Slaughtercult symbolizes a conspiracy for raw black metal!"

Repeating one of the most pervasive themes in all metal, Oneilar goes on to say "the greatest influence for music is occultism. The 'magic' within our thoughts which forms validity in Slaughtercult's music." And while she has written and sung some seriously brutal lyrics, when asked in the same interview what she would do with only one day to live, her answer was poetic:

"I'd spend the last remaining time within the Polish woods amongst those few worthy individuals, which have accompanied me on my path in loyalty. There the last Darkened Nocturn of Slaughtercult would be celebrated. Right before the wind's scraggy, bony pinions carry me away...as the track "Underneath Stars of the East" resounds for all eternity..."

****

Moving into the 21st century, black metal branched off into new forms and mixed with old forms in the ever-shifting kaleidoscope of genres. It also became more woman-friendly. Black metal bands that are all-female or female-fronted are not as rare as they once were, and can be found all over the globe. Gallhammer, a two-woman band formed in Tokyo in 2003, play a doomy, crusty version of black metal more akin to punk than anything atmospheric, and are becoming known for the wailing, dark, and relentless quality of their music.

"I don't really care about us being unusual just because we are women," said vocalist and bassist Vivian Slaughter in an interview with *jaME-World*. "I enjoy playing black metal, but I don't have any big ambitions to be successful, I want to just enjoy playing with my band. Recently a lot of young people play in bands, and I don't think there's a big difference between a man and a woman who play in a band." But she opened up further concerning her musical intentions to *Cosmic Lava* in 2004, saying, "I wanted to express the mental instability and mental cruelty which a girl has." With this boldly honest statement, she puts herself and fellow band member Risa Reaper squarely in the black/death metal tradition of exposing and examining subjects that are hidden or off-limits.

Paring the number down even further is

Anguished, a one-woman black metal band from Finland. Possessed Demoness is the woman behind Anguished, which she created in 2009, and with the exception of using a session drummer, she does all the vocals and other instrumentation herself. Her vocal quality has been described as "tormented and intense," and words such as "depressive" and "melancholy" are attached to her music.

On the cover of her 2010 album, *Cold*, she is shown from the back wearing a thong and fishnet stockings, and the image she cultivates is part corpse-paint, part pin-up, and deliberately provocative, traditionally a component of the extreme metal ethos. Her mixture of darkness, sex, and sadness is unique, but her source of inspiration seems almost universal in metal. "I worship Satan," she told Canadian Assault zine. "I live the way of Black Metal and that includes Satanic and occultic things."

****

Since ancient times, women have been thought to hold great power and magic, mainly due to their mystery and connection with the moon, the earth, and the cycle of birth and death. Because there is a side of black metal that is an affirmation of earth worship and a celebration of the dark and mysterious, it is naturally attractive to women. Black metal may have been created by men, but women now have the power to give it a new and richer life.

Photo of Versklaven by Sarja Hasan

Chapter Seven

Tourniquet:

Women in Symphonic Metal

I tried to kill my pain
But only brought more
So much more
I lay dying
And I'm pouring crimson regret and betrayal
I'm dying, praying, bleeding and screaming
Am I too lost to be saved?
Am I too lost?

My God my tourniquet
Return to me salvation

My God my tourniquet
Return to me salvation

Do you remember me?
Lost for so long
Will you be on the other side
Or will you forget me?
I'm dying, praying, bleeding and screaming
Am I too lost to be saved?
Am I too lost?
  - Evanescence, "Tourniquet" – *Fallen*

"In influencing and often initiating social changes and inspiring men to produce new music for new occasions, the priestess of beauty had a mission....Through her, music came to be regarded as one of the direct functions of a lady."
  -Sophie Drinker, *Music and Women*

Symphonic metal, also known as operatic metal (or more derogatorily, corset metal) can refer to any type of metal that incorporates elements of classical music, such as orchestral instruments or chorus vocals. The genre has roots in progressive metal, a blend of the compositional complexity and instrumental variety of progressive rock with the technicality and ferocity of thrash, made famous in the 1990s by bands like Queensrÿche and Dream Theater, and later embraced by Nightwish, Therion, and a host of others. The new millennium brought more innovation, as bands such as Lacuna Coil, Leave's Eyes, After Forever, and Edenbridge were born, all with one thing in common: they were fronted by women who sang in an operatic style and whose voices were in the soprano or mezzo-soprano range. This formula of a female singer with a beautiful, often classically-trained voice in front of an all-male metal band was so successful that the terms "operatic" and "symphonic" have become virtually interchangeable, even though operatic metal is technically a sub-genre under the symphonic heading. Some bands also accentuated vocal contrast by adding male death growls to the singer's soprano, in a style often referred to as "beauty and the beast."

Evanescence is by far one of the best-known examples of this kind of music in America. The band plays a slightly more rock-oriented and radio-friendly version of operatic metal, and their frontwoman is the talented vocalist and classically-trained pianist Amy Lee. Formed in 1995 by Amy and guitarist Ben Moody, they broke into the mainstream in 2003 with their debut album *Fallen*, featuring the hit songs "Bring Me to Life," "Going Under," and "My Immortal." Many in the metal scene, both here and abroad, were bemused when American popular music embraced Evanescence as something new and different, since the band essentially followed the same formula as dozens of other symphonic metal bands, many of them with large followings in Europe and Asia. *Fallen* went on to sell 17 million copies, and the group became an unstoppable force in the early 2000s, receiving multiple Grammy nominations and platinum records.

Amy Lee became a worldwide celebrity, and as a result, a representative of all women in heavy music and an ambassador of sorts to middle-of-the-road listeners. But Evanescence was plagued by lineup changes, including co-founder Ben Moody's mid-tour departure in 2003, and after releasing two more records, the band went on hiatus in 2009. Their long-awaited third studio album came out in 2011, and another is reported to be in the works.

In a 2012 interview with *AltSounds*, she responded to the inevitable question about the experience of being a woman in a man's industry by saying that it had actually worked to her advantage by making the band stand out. She ended her answer with, "I don't try not to be female; I don't try to prove that I'm hard." The interviewer then pointed out that although Amy is a metal musician and a feminist, she is "completely feminine and kind of delicate." The implied contradictions in that statement are perhaps one reason this particular brand of metal appealed to a wider audience; there was a fascination not only with the novelty of a female singer, but also with the contrast created by a lovely young woman with a lilting voice against a background of menacing male figures, not to mention the inherent conflict between feminism and the headbanger stereotype. Amy's response to the *AltSounds* interviewer was to the point: "I believe it [the rock industry] needs an infusion of femininity because for me, music is music. More than anything, it's just about being taken seriously as a strong musician, as an artist, and not as a gimmick." More recently, Amy has also been working on some solo music, and she just announced she is expecting her first child. In June 2014, she gave the MTV News website a hint of what to expect from the band's upcoming album. "I think it's gonna be kinda spooky," she said. "I'd like to use more organ. I wanna make it heavier and softer at the same time."

****

After Forever, one of the heaviest bands in symphonic metal, formed in 1995 as a death metal band, ultimately changing their sound when Dutch vocalist Floor Jansen joined the band in 1997. They started to incorporate symphonic elements into their music, and over the years developed a stronger progressive influence. The group stayed together until 2009 with a few lineup changes, and recorded five studio albums. When they disbanded, Floor wasted no time starting her own group, ReVamp, in addition to taking over vocal duties for Nightwish. She also collaborated on many side projects and made guest appearances with other bands of various genres. Her versatility as a vocalist has kept her in high demand; she is a trained soprano who can also do guttural death growls and aggressive screams.

In interviews, she usually deflects questions about gender by saying that she has always felt accepted among male musicians, and states that in her career she encountered only a minimal amount of sexism. As she told *BraveWords* in 2013, she advocates a genderless classification of music. "If all women keep emphasizing that there is a big difference between females and men in metal, that's not getting to an equal position – that's emphasizing differences …by dividing the female and male worlds – even by using the name 'female fronted metal' – says nothing about the music, nothing about the singing or the quality of it, and I think it should start with that."

****

Another famous figure on the underground side of operatic metal is Liv Kristine, formerly of the Norwegian band Theatre of Tragedy, and currently the vocalist for Leave's Eyes. She joined Theatre of Tragedy in 1994, and quickly moved from backup singer to frontwoman, making hers one of the earliest "clean" voices heard in the extreme metal world. In 2003, after being unceremoniously fired by Theatre of Tragedy, she joined forces with the German death metal group Atrocity, calling the new band Leave's Eyes. That same year she married Atrocity vocalist Alexander Krull and gave birth to their son. Unlike Kimberly Goss, a metal vocalist who chose to exit the scene when she became a mother, Liv enjoys keeping the family together by taking her young son with her when she and her husband are on tour with Leave's Eyes.

In 2010, she wrote a post for *Decibel* magazine's blog, entitled "Top 5 Reasons Why Women in Metal Rule." Her first reason is "Women in metal don't lose their jobs when they become mothers," and the last one is quite direct: "Women in metal are special. Women in metal are still heavily outnumbered by males. Therefore we get more attention." The list made it clear that women were appreciated in the symphonic metal scene, and showed how female-oriented the climate of this genre had become in a relatively short amount of time.

****

Symphonic metal has its critics, but the rapid proliferation of bands in this genre, coupled with the enormous success of a handful of groups at the top, proves that it is here to stay. Certainly, one benefit to women in metal has been simply the increase in their number and visibility, but more importantly, their options have increased as well. They no longer have to follow the dictates of record companies or imitate male musicians to be accepted, and they are not required to hide or ignore their womanhood, or pretend that they agree with the notion that femininity equals weakness. The courageous women of this genre deserve credit for turning the tide of metal domination, but praise is also due the men who stand behind them, on and off the stage.

Photo of Scizophasia by Sarja Hasan

Chapter Eight

Boys in Dresses: Genderbending and Grindcore

"I learned that boys in dresses are OK on the last day of school.
There was a rainbow like a halo over the world."
        - Pig Destroyer, "Scatology Homework" – *Prowler in the Yard*

        "The supreme example among goddesses is Artemis. She represents at once the creative individual who meets life with a proud, positive attitude and the creative freedom of collective womanhood ...reflecting the value placed by the

ancients on womanhood as an independent spiritual power."
    -Sophie Drinker, *Music and Women*

Grindcore is a genre closely related to death metal, since the two developed alongside each other in England and the United States. Napalm Death, the pioneering British grindcore band, played fast, chaotic music with all the chops of death metal, but took their cues from the early punk movement instead of horror movies or Satanism. They set the stage for a genre that valued equality and diversity alongside brutality and extremity. Despite being all-male, these bands were espousing an ethos that seemed to echo the rhetoric of gay and women's rights; Warsore, an early grind band from Australia, sang "You Rape, You Die," Napalm Death wrote the ironic "It's a M.A.N.S. World," and grind veterans Brutal Truth penned "Anti-Homophobe."

Women in this scene were few at first, but they were definitely there. New York's Nausea formed in 1985, with Amy Miret on vocals. They are one of the many bands that straddle genre, falling somewhere between grindcore, doom, and d-beat punk, or crust. One remarkable thing about Nausea is that there wasn't a big deal made out of the fact that there was a woman in an extreme band as early as the 80s; the scene was geared towards political correctness, and as such, created a space for women to be true equals to men.

Flagitious Idiosyncrasy in the Dilapidation, an all-female Japanese grind band formed in 2001, is an unusual musical project and one notable example of the experimentation that is part of this scene. Although all three band members were involved in other extreme metal projects at the time of their formation, they left their respective bands to realize the vision of forming a female grindcore group. Shortly after releasing a demo, FID got signed to underground grind label Leprous Bizarre Productions, and have since released a full-length album. FID are known for their piercing shrieks, incredibly fast playing, and pummeling guitar-and-percussion assault. Despite the fact that they play noisy, chaotic music, they are all accomplished musicians and masters of their respective instruments.

Another talented example is Canada's Mares of Thrace. Started by Thérèse Lanz and Stefani MacKichan in 2009, Mares of Thrace are a two-woman noise/grind/doom/post-hardcore duo who don't play by anyone's rules. What they do play is a blend of sludgy and depressed grind that showcases their artistic sensibilities as well as aggressive musical skill. In July of 2013, Stefani, the drummer, left the band to pursue her studies, and was replaced by Rae Amity, another female metal drummer. In a 2013 interview for this book, she stated that the new duo will continue to record music and tour, despite the fact that Thérèse is also busy working as a computer programmer.

Similar to FID, Thérèse and her counterparts are fashionable and feminine, but this is not how they define their identity as a band. On their Facebook page, Thérèse pokes fun at female fashion aesthetics in metal, commenting on a photo of herself in a pretty dress and a leather jacket: "I was once told 'You can't play metal in a pink dress.' Oh I can't, can't I?" She also frequently reposts and supports other female musicians and women's rights issues, and has a high standard for female representation in the press. Her response to the group's inclusion in *Decibel* Magazine's "Women in Metal" issue was this: "Well, it might be in the smallest font on the bottom row, but our name's still on the cover of *Decibel*. Also, props to *Decibel* for having an issue on women in metal in which women are referred to as 'women' and everyone is wearing clothes."

When asked about her level of comfort in the grind scene in an interview for this book, Thérèse responded, "In terms of comfort, I'm generally a bit more comfortable at the crossover genre shows with someone passing out pro-choice and animal rights pamphlets, than at the pornogrind shows with bands playing that have names like 'Twat Rammer' or whatever." She also agrees that there is an overwhelming amount of positivity to be found in the scene, although she laments the prejudices that still face women playing heavy music. "People should think about what they're really saying when they say stuff like our record was 'surprisingly' good, our drummer 'actually' has really proficient drum chops, etc."

****

Mel Mongeon, singer for the Canadian grindcore band Fuck the Facts, is a vocalist with an earsplitting grindcore scream and amazing range, and also a bilingual songwriter; French is her first language, but she wrote lyrics in English until a few years ago when she decided to include her native tongue. Her partner Topon Das, the band's founder and guitarist, had this to say about the change: "If she wanted to write every song in French from here on out, she has my blessing. Besides, with the genre of music we are playing, and with all the screaming, I'm pretty sure the majority of people can't even really tell the difference if you are screaming in English or you are screaming in French."

Fuck the Facts started in 1998, and Mel officially joined in 2002. Known for the volume and intensity of her grind vocals, Mel continued performing while pregnant with her daughter. Her response to the usual woman-in-metal question – this time in a 2013 interview with *DarkMedia* – was: "It is not an issue and it is not something I think about," but she did go on to add a few details of life on the road. "I'm not someone that needs a super high level of comfort, so shitty bathroom, smelly vans and scummy clubs don't scare me."

In a 2013 interview with *Underworld*, her bandmate, drummer Mathieu Vilandre, was asked how having a female vocalist had impacted Fuck the Facts. "We get that question a lot," he said. "Within the band, it doesn't change anything. It makes people talk a lot, that's for sure, and Mel sometimes has to deal with creepy dudes. I would hope that it inspires other female artists to go ahead with their passion and give it all they've got."

Katherine Katz, formerly of the doom band

Salome, has appeared as a guest vocalist with such well-known grindcore bands as Pig Destroyer and Agoraphobic Nosebleed. Kat has one of the most powerful voices in grindcore, and like Mel Mongeon, she is petite. Her height of just over five feet is often remarked upon in interviews; even *The New York Times* couldn't resist calling her "a small woman with small hands" in an appreciative 2010 review, which included a more descriptive passage about her live performance: "She becomes transparent, and music flows through her …It's rare to see someone rock this way, top to bottom, inside and out. It doesn't necessarily mean provoking your crowd or being an acrobat. It means giving yourself completely to your task.

Kitty Play Records prefaced an interview with Kat by calling her "a focused vocalist who screams from the mind." When asked if the metal scene was sexist, she didn't hold back, replying in part, "If you are a good vocalist, you're only good for a woman. For however long you're involved in metal, you will be acknowledged as a female vocalist, instead of a vocalist …If you dress too feminine, if you look too sexy, if you have anything besides dark hair, you will most likely be seen as a gimmick. If you behave more on the masculine side, you will be seen as a fake, trying too hard …Your appearance will be mentioned repeatedly."

****

Cretin came onto the scene in 1992, playing a blistering blend of death metal and grindcore with intelligent lyrics and ripping guitar riffs. Inspired by death metal legends Repulsion, who wrote fast, punk-tinged songs about the reality of death, Cretin were one of the first groups to play what would come to be known as deathgrind. They had a good reputation in the grindcore community, but weren't seen as especially unique until 2008, when Dan, the three-piece band's vocalist and guitarist, came out as a transgendered individual. Although he was known as a hairy, masculine headbanger at the time, he was never comfortable with this image, and longed to be seen as a female. He came out to the metal community in an issue of *Decibel* Magazine, announcing that it was too hard for him to go on living as a man, and that he intended to divorce his wife, go through gender therapy, and undergo a sex change to officially transition from Dan Martinez to Marissa Martinez.

Marissa was not sure how fans would react to her new persona. "Honestly, I had no idea if I would be accepted," she admitted in an interview with *Invisible Oranges*. "I imagined a lot of people laughing and joking about it. But I kind of just threw caution to the wind. And this was before I even did the gender transition. I felt a little bit stuck because I just didn't want to quit the band. I love my band. But it was something I had to do, so I didn't think about the reaction."

She would soon realize she had little to worry about. The news was welcomed by extreme music journalists, who all wanted a piece of the action via interview, and applauded by many fans, from die-hard Cretin enthusiasts to other transgendered people in the underground metal community who looked to her as an inspiration and role model. Some cited these Cretin lyrics as evidence that Marissa had been suppressing her gender identity for a long time:

> *I didn't want a son*
> *I got one anyway*
> *Little boys have nasty*
> *Things between their legs*
> *I'd rather have a girl*
> *A dolly I can dress*
> *My pretty little princess*
> *A transgender success*

Daddy's little girl
Daddy's little girl
Dressing him in drag
He's confused and kind of sad
Daddy's little girl
Daddy's little girl
Teaching him to be
A little she and not a he

- Cretin, "Daddy's Little Girl" – *Freakery*

Since her successful sex change, Marissa has rejoined Cretin, taken over vocal duties, and even gotten the once-in-a-lifetime chance to play guitar in Repulsion, the pioneering grind band that inspired her to play extreme music in the first place.

Thérèse Lanz of Mares of Thrace had this to say when asked for a response about Marissa: "I am fiercely (overbearingly, even!) LGBT-positive. Trans people are currently roughly where gay people were 30 years ago, in terms of public understanding and acceptance, and Marissa is a bad-ass for transitioning unapologetically and relatively publicly. I hope she inspires other trans people in metal to do the same. As for people's reactions… hah, when it comes to transgender, I try and ignore people's reactions. Ostensibly hip and liberal young people say the most ignorant shit about trans people all the time, and I've referred so many people to the American Psychological Association's website on the topic, in order to shut them up, that I have that shit bookmarked."

****

       Grindcore, with its emphasis on equality and social awareness, is a scene where women and men can feel free to incorporate feminist ideals into their music if they choose. The attitudes and culture of this genre reflect Sophie Drinker's description of ancient civilizations in the time of what she calls "the great goddesses": "Worshiping nature's rhythmic laws and striving to keep in touch with the life force …men and women set a spiritual value on woman's natural way. Men and women both lived according to the principle that woman is creative in body and spirit." (*Music and Women*, pp. 122-3) Tolerance of differences and respect for rights may be characteristic of grindcore's lifestyle and lyrics, but the music itself is anything but peace-loving. Singing and playing this fast and aggressive form of music can be an outlet for aggression as well as a way of connecting with the primitive self, and from grindcore's early years to the present, women have proven that they deserve their place on the stage.

Photo of Varix by Sarja Hasan

Chapter Nine

Return of the Goddess:

Women in Today's Doom Metal

The season of the witch is autumn long
Weird silence falls upon the throng
They smoke black drugs with Saturn's bong
And blast our mind with evil song
I see witches in the sky
Flying toward a Quaalude eye

Visions of light from the demon's sun
Goat-headed serfs drink to this dawn
A strange vintage brewed in casks oblong

In a perfumed black mass with reptile gongs

- Blood Ceremony, "Into the Coven," –
Blood Ceremony

Male heavy metal music started in the late 60s when some rock bands decided to write sinister-sounding music about Satan; for women, it started with Jinx Dawson and Coven. Because Jinx as a young woman in an industry dominated by men was confident enough to start her own band, playing heavy music with a satanic theme, the door was opened for a generation of women rockers in the 70s and 80s New Wave of British Heavy Metal scene, and it has remained open through the years and the proliferation of genres that followed.

However, while Jinx and her group may have been a big influence on bands of their time, psychedelic-influenced metal, or doom, practically disappeared in the later 70s, making way for hypermasculinized bands like Iron Maiden and Judas Priest. For years the trend in metal was to play as loud and as fast as possible, resulting in new developments like death metal, black metal, thrash, speed metal, and grindcore. Doom may have fallen out of fashion, but it never really went away. Newer bands are finding ways to pay homage to the past without seeming trite or derivative, and adding some fresh ingredients to the nefarious brew of classic doom.

****

In the early 1980s, a new generation picked up on the original Black Sabbath sound and made some music of their own. U.S. bands, in addition to the notorious Pentagram, included Sorcery, Saint Vitus, and Trouble. In Europe, groups like Pagan Altar, Witchfinder General, Candlemass, Cathedral, and Count Raven joined the scene. All were inspired by the metal of bygone years, when the music was slow and heavy, and the lyrics were dark. Vocalist Scott Weinrich of Saint Vitus penned the song "Born Too Late" in 1986, bemoaning the fact that he wasn't old enough in the late 60s and early 70s to fully enjoy the heyday of doom.

Not only was he born too late, he was also born a little too early. The doom metal phenomenon would take off again, but not for a few more years. New groups began to appear in the 90s, and the early 2000s saw the genre making a huge comeback. Influenced by the post-punk and grunge scene, bands such as The Melvins and Mudhoney gave traditional doom a new lease on life with a form of doom often classified as sludge metal, a sub-sub-genre of metal. In another sub-genre, stoner metal, bands with names like Weedeater and Bongzilla typically play a doomy fusion of metal, rock, and country. There were death metal/doom and black metal/doom combos, as genre lines blurred and scenes became interchangeable with one another. But however it was classified, doom had made a comeback, and it remains a popular segment of the metal scene today.

As this brand of music made its triumphant return, so did the imagery of paganism, witchcraft, and sorcery. Some of this symbolism was already present in black metal, but doom's particular mixture of paganism and psychedelia speaks even more to the goddess tradition. Doom bands of the early 2000s, such as Gates of Slumber, Grand Magus, and Witchcraft, were all male, but it didn't take long for groups with female members to emerge. The Third and The Mortal, a Norwegian band, blended harsh, abrasive doom with clean vocals and guitar by their female singer, Kari Rueslåtten. The band went on to play more experimental types of metal, and they have been cited as an inspiration for the gothic metal scene, the modern-day doom scene, and the jazz-influenced experimental metal scene as well.

In the early years of the 21st century, women became inspired by the music of Coven, The Third and the Mortal, and by many all-male doom bands as well, to form a sub-sub-genre of their own which has come to be known as female-fronted doom metal. One such band, Monarch!, have risen to underground fame despite the challenge of having members in four different countries, and having to get together yearly in Japan to write and record music. Monarch! have a sludgy, atmospheric sound, and are driven by the screams, shrieks and chants of vocalist Emilie Bresson. Although she loves traveling the world playing music, she has met with her share of trouble due to her gender. "When I first started, it was sometimes difficult because the more macho dudes didn't think girls had their place in the metal scene," she told *Decibel* Magazine in their "Women in Metal" issue.

"Well, not on stage, anyways, I have had my fair share of guys trying to grab me while onstage, telling me to fuck off, and have been the subject of some incredibly sexist write-ups. But whatever, I'm here for the music, and that has never stopped me from doing what I love."

There does seem to be some lingering sexism from the so-called purists in the doom scene, but fortunately, there are plenty of female-fronted groups to counteract this mentality. Blood Ceremony, in aesthetic quite similar to Coven, combine satanic lyrics and imagery with a psychedelic, Jethro Tull-inspired flavor to create a unique and creepy blend. Vocalist Alia O'Brien, who also plays flute and organ, offered her opinion on the prevalence of women in doom and occult rock during an interview with *Canada Arts Connect*: "It might have something to do with the fact that the sources of lyrical inspiration in these genres are riddled with female archetypes, like the old crone, the high priestess, but I would hate to jump to conclusions."

Wooden Stake, a death/doom duo consisting of Vanessa Nocera on guitar and vocals and Wayne Sarantopoulus on drums, focus on witchcraft and the occult in songs with titles such as "Salem, 1692" and "Skullcoven." Witch Mountain, another woman-fronted group, started in 1997 as a male three-piece. Since Uta Plotkin was invited to join as lead singer in 2009, they have ruled the scene with haunting female vocals on two successful albums, *South of Salem* and *Cauldron of the Wild*. In 2007, a psych doom band from Wisconsin called Totem rechristened itself Jex Thoth, which happens to be the name of its female vocalist, and have recently released an album with the woman-centric title *Blood Moon Rise*. Other notable examples are Acid King, a doomy stoner/psych/rock band with Lori S. on vocals, Christian Mistress, a Seattle-based old-school metal band with singer Christine Davis, and Windhand of Richmond, Virginia, a classic doom band with Dorthia Cottrell as the singer.

Most of the females in this scene are frontwomen of their groups, but there are exceptions. Emily Witch, bassist of the old-school British doom band Witchsorrow, wears jeans instead of the ceremonial costumes favored by some, and while she doesn't see herself as the face of the band, or of the macabre aesthetic, she does see doom as a viable outlet for female musicians. "The gang mentality of bands appeals to boys," she told Decibel. "They're quite happy sitting in a garage fiddling around with instruments, whereas girls want to be out and about doing things. Boys form these gangs quite early on, and it's difficult for girls to infiltrate that. You have to be very keen and be prepared to be accepted on your own merits. You definitely have to have something to prove. There are rules, and metal can feel closed off to outsiders. Maybe that's why women struggle with it. But the doom scene is more mature, and possibly this makes it easier to be a woman in a doom band. It's not all teenage boys baying for blood and boobs."

Emily is happy to see this surge of female power in the metal scene, especially within doom. "It's a different dynamic," she says. "They're less under suspicion of being there as afterthoughts or a marketing trick." She also doesn't understand why women in metal bands are expected to use sex to sell. "I've never been to a gig and thought, 'I wish that guy had taken his shirt off!' I'm all for theater in metal, but it's gotta be pitched right. We have theatrical elements, but getting my clothes off isn't one of them."

Electric Wizard is another doom band with a woman member who is not the vocalist. Although they formed in 1995, Liz Buckingham didn't join the group until 2003, when she was asked by band founder Jus Oborn to replace their original guitarist. In terms of being respected as a female metal musician, she has had her share of issues. In 2011, National Public Radio's music news site described her as both "a bastion of understated, self-confident strength and femininity" and "a leather-clad, self-taught axeslinger who brought one of metal's most important bands back from the brink with her leaden riffs."

"When I first got involved in the metal scene, it was very male-oriented/dominated." Liz told NPR. "There were hardly ever any girls in the audience, let alone onstage, whereas today, I definitely see a lot more girls into metal and playing it than back then. But despite that, I don't really see that the playing field has leveled out – maybe a tiny bit. I think I personally deal with a little less of it now just because I'm in a better-known band now and I've been playing for so long. When I first started, it was very hard to gain respect in the metal world, and I feel like it's still pretty much the same."

       Women in the current doom scene are more likely to be honest when questioned about gender issues than their predecessors in the era of record-label tyranny. "The way some men think about women has a lot more to do with their upbringing than the amount of women playing guitar in metal bands." Liz adds. "So it will be a very long time, if ever, that things will change that much. Maybe it will – or has become – less acceptable to outright treat women with disrespect, but it's not going to change certain individuals' way of thinking, no matter how much they suppress it or [how much it] is considered socially unacceptable."

****

       Denver's Dead Temple are a group with three female singers who personify the goddess tradition in their onstage attire and their approach to lyrics and music. They were eager to speak about this trend in heavy metal, and shared some insight on the topic in an interview for this book. "There's no doubt we're seeing a rise of women in heavy music doing the witchy thing," said Jade Morgan, one of the three vocalists. "We're in no way pioneers of this style. We owe a lot to bands like Jex Thoth, Christian Mistress, Witch Mountain, Jess and the Ancient Ones, Acid King, Blood Ceremony, The Devil's Blood, etc. They've created a facet in new heavy music where women have a more level playing field to narrate and exorcise some dark energy. What's great is this also seems to be a resurgence of proto-metal and traditional doom. It's excellent to see women in bands that pay homage to groups that gave birth to doom and metal – bands like Coven, Black Sabbath, Pentagram, Captain Beyond, Black Widow, Sir Lord Baltimore, Pagan Altar, Dust, Candlemass, etc. Historically, aggressive music has been a place for the undesirables and discriminated-against (including women) to have a voice, turn the tables, and rattle some cages... I think we're seeing a return to fundamentals in a spooky package – where there are more women on stage and not just men dressed in their clothes."

****

Overall, women in the doom scene seem to have more agency than in any other sub-genre in the history of metal. In this arena, women can sing, but they can also play guitar; similarly, a band can have a name with "witch" in the title and play earth-centric music, even without a woman in the band. Women have the creative control not only to write music and lyrics, but to choose the band's image and messages as well. As it was with Jinx Dawson and Coven in the beginning, in today's doom bands, the founders and leaders are often the female member or members. Although some gender issues in the doom scene are still unresolved, it seems to be the most comfortable and nurturing genre for women in metal thus far. The ladies of doom are thriving, and their numbers are growing every day.

At the end of *Music and Women*, Sophie

Drinker discusses her belief that women will regain their rightful place in society as healers, guides, and musicians, using their experiences as females – the good and the bad – to help define their art. "They must find rituals and music to reinforce their own spirits in the crises of womanhood," she writes. "And they must have representation in the larger life of the community for the authority of the natural woman; then can the Daughters of the Moon proceed boldly and confidently to the task of objectifying their experiences in whatever way they find opportunity and incentive."

Sophie Drinker originally intended "Daughters of the Moon" as the title of her book. If she were alive today, she might not recognize some of the forms that female musicianship has taken, but she would surely find pride and validation in the accomplishments of the wicked women of heavy metal.

Here, Queen Goddess, light-bringer, divine Moon,
Who move in a path of night, wandering in the
darkness.
Torch-bearer of the mysteries, Moon-maiden, rich
in stars,
You who gave and diminish, who are both female
and
male,
All-seeing, enlightener, fruit-bearer, Mother of
Time,
Splendor of amber, soulful, illuminator, you who
are Birth.
Lover of all-night wakefulness, fountain of beautiful

stars!
Whose joy is the tranquil silence of the blissful
spirit of night
The lustrous one, giver of charms, votive statue of
night,
You who bring fruit to perfection, visions and
sacred rites!
Queen of stars, in flowing veils, who move on a
curving path,
All-wise maiden, blessed one, keeper of the treasury
of stars,
May you come in beautiful gladness, shining in all
your brilliance;
And saving the youthful suppliants who turn to you,
Maiden Moon!

- Orphic hymn, from *Music and Women*

Conclusion:

Season of the Witch

It is difficult, if not completely impossible, to draw strict conclusions about the overall role of women in the metal scene. There are multiple genres and branches of heavy metal, each containing women as different from each other as women in hip-hop are from women in country music, and truthfully, there is no all-encompassing answer to the question of where and how women fit into this world. Some frontwomen realize that success depends as much on their looks as on their voices, and they like it that way. Others are guitar prodigies who downplay their appearance. And still others throw all stereotypes to the wind and just do what makes them happy, even if that means they don't fit comfortably into any particular scene and reap the benefits of that association. It isn't entirely accurate to say that women in heavy metal have come only so far, or are stuck in this or that position, because there are so many varied parts to be played, not to mention so many different definitions of metal. However, it is clear that women who choose to play in these bands have a lot more to consider than men who make the same choice.

But back in 1969, Jinx Dawson, a college

student and trained vocalist, didn't worry about the implications of joining the metal scene, because there was no scene. She felt she could sing her heart out about Satan and the earth, embrace her womanhood and sexuality along with her masculine side, and be comfortable within herself as a person and an artist; judging by the evidence of her sustained presence, she still does. And with the resurgence in popularity of doom metal, women have again found a place in the scene that doesn't focus on gender politics or thrive on controversy. In the doom metal of today, women can wear velvet cloaks or denim jackets; they can play guitar, or flute, or drums, or be the singer, or do any combination of these things. And they can sing about witchcraft and magic, the earth and Satan, and appeal to both genders, as they celebrate the female energy of the earth and the traditionally masculine ethos of heaviness and evil.

I hope you have enjoyed this book and learned something about women in the metal scene. Whether you are a feminist, a metalhead, or both, I hope this book has taught you something new and piqued your interest about a band or an idea.

Acknowledgements

Thanks to my mom, Ann Dexter Androla, not only for raising me and always encouraging me no matter what, but also for tirelessly editing this book with me, and helping me look at things from the perspective of a metalhead, a feminist, a woman, and a mom.

Thanks also to Hannah Swann for doing the amazing cover art for this book, as well as the great illustrations, and helping me with promotion. Sarja Hassan deserves tons of praise for providing photography for this project, promoting, and giving us a shout-out in *Maximum Rock n' Roll*! The ladies in Dead Temple were kind enough to answer all my interview questions, proof the book, help with promotion and sales, and just generally help a recent Denver transplant feel at home. Thérèse from Mares of Thrace, thank you for answering some questions for me despite your busy schedule, and thanks to Kerry from Occultist, Graham Scala, and the countless other amazing women and men who helped with and contributed to this book. And thanks to Wil Wilson, my partner, for supporting me, providing insight, and encouraging me to finish this book.

Lastly, thank you to all the amazing publications in Denver, Richmond, and the metal and feminist scenes who have provided or will provide coverage and promotion for this book. And of course, to all the women I wrote about, Jinx Dawson especially. You are the inspiration for this project!

Appendix

Chapter One
-Jinx Dawson and Coven:
http://forums.stevehoffman.tv/threads/nice-new-article-on-jinx-dawson-from-coven.132920/
-http://wnyu.org/2008-02-11_plastictalesfrommarshmallowdimension - great live interview!

Chapter Two
-The book Running with the Devil: Power, Gender and Madness in Heavy Metal Music by Robert Walser was a great help to me, it's one of the few academic books on metal and gender out there!
-http://www.metalmaidens.com/bitch.htm - interview with Betsy Bitch
-Feminist Legal Theory Blogspot on Glam Metal – link no longer available
http://technorati.com/entertainment/music/article/interview-doro-pesch-heavy-metal-goddess/ - Doro Pescch/Warlock Interview

Chapter Three
-www.blueoystercult.com - Info on Patti Smith and Blue Oyster Cult
-https://www.youtube.com/watch?v=PLQM84ucMPU – Interview with Wendy O Williams on Night

Flight

https://www.facebook.com/pages/Plasmatics/276891670976?sk=info – info on Plasmatics' background

Chapter Four

-http://www.examiner.com/review/lita-ford-interview-a-runaway-who-became-the-electric-queen-of-rock-and-metal - Examiner interview with Lita Ford

-http://steelandfire.20m.com/annint.html - Ann Boleyn interview with Steel and Fire

http://femmemetalwebzine.tumblr.com/post/27186531514/interview-sabina-classen-olli-jaath-holy-moses – Holy Moses interview

-http://www.rockeyez.com/interviews/int-great-kat.html - Rock Eyez interview with The Great Kat

http://www.unratedmagazine.com/Document.cfm?Page=Articles/index.cfm&Article_ID=798 – Chastain interview with Unrated Magazine

Chapter Five

- http://www.invisibleoranges.com/2011/05/are-you-talking-to-me-respecting-women-in-metal/ - Invisible Oranges on respecting women in metal

- http://www.metalsucks.net/2012/11/26/future-ex-mrs-axl-rosenberg-quits-cerebral-bore/ - Metalsucks article about Simone quitting Cerebral Bore

http://www.blistering.com/fastpage/fpengine.php/templateid/29474/menuid/3/tempidx/5/link/1 – Interview with Paul from Cerebral Bore

-Haemorrhage interview on Infernal Domain – blog currently unavailable

-Choosing Death by Albert Mudrain – quotes from Jo Bench of Bolt Thrower and Angela Gossow of Arch Enemy

-http://feministheadbanger.wordpress.com/page/4/ - Ms. Anthropia on violence in death metal lyrics – check out the blog, she is great!

Chapter Six

-http://www.metalmaidens.com/sinergy.htm - interview with Kimberly Goss

-http://www.lordsofmetal.nl/en/interviews/view/id/523 - interview with Onilear

Chapter Seven

-http://hangout.altsounds.com/features/153489-lowdown-interview-amy-lee-evanescence.html - AltSounds interview with Amy Lee of Evanescence

-Deciblog's Top 5 Reasons Why Women in Metal Rule – currently unavailable, although you can read the list paraphrased many other places on the internet

-http://feministheadbanger.wordpress.com/page/4/ - Ms. Anthropia on the Top 5 Reasons Why Women in Metal Rule

http://www.feministezine.com/feminist/corset_feminist.html - Suzanne Macnevin examines the corset in a feminist context

http://thefemalevoices.blogspot.com/p/symphonic-metal-history.html - the history of symphonic metal
        -http://www.metal-rules.com/metalnews/2013/11/24/floor-jansen/ - Interview with Floor Jansen

Chapter Eight
-https://www.facebook.com/maresofthraceca - wisdom from Thérèse Lanz
        -Some of my quotes from Thérèse Lanz are directly from an interview I did with her
        -http://www.invisibleoranges.com/2011/01/interview-marissa-martinez-cretin/ - Invisible Oranges interview with Marissa Martinez
        -http://www.terrorizer.com/news/features-2/miranda-s-interview-with-grind-frontwoman-marissa-martinez/ - Terrorizor's online Marissa Martinez interview

Chapter Nine
-Decibel's "Women in Metal" Issue
-My interview with the ladies in Dead Temple

        * All lyrics are from CD lyric booklets, *darklyrics.com*, or *lyricsfreak.com*. Check out these sites to find lyrics to almost every metal song, ever

        **Wikipedia* and *Encyclopedia Metallum* were both used as references to verify information in this book and find links to other sources.

However, they were never used as primary or sole sources of information.

***For all chapters of this book, I consulted *Music and Women* by Sophie Drinker. Originally published in 1948, this book tells some very wonderful stories of female singers and musicians throughout history before women's lib was fully realized. If you dig anthropology, feminism, or music, check this out!

***Cover image is Kerry Zylstra of Occultist and Dominique Withoff of Versklaven. Occultist are a blackened punk/metal band from Richmond, VA. Versklaven are a metal-influenced punk band from Houston, TX.

23301009R00062

Made in the USA
Middletown, DE
15 December 2018